Freshwater Fishing

By Ryan Gale

childsworld.com

Published by The Child's World®
800-599-READ • www.childsworld.com

Photography Credits
Photographs ©: Jeff Feverston/Shutterstock Images, cover, 1; iStockphoto, 5, 6, 20; Vlad Sokolovsky/Shutterstock Images, 9; Shutterstock Images, 10, 11 (fish), 16 (lures), 19; Roman Chazov/Shutterstock Images, 13; Sean F Boggs/iStockphoto, 15; Aaron/L.A. Photography/Shutterstock Images, 17; Jozef Durok/iStockphoto, 21

ISBN Information
9781503869745 (Reinforced Library Binding)
9781503881013 (Portable Document Format)
9781503882324 (Online Multi-user eBook)
9781503883635 (Electronic Publication)

LCCN 2022951134

Printed in the United States of America

ABOUT THE AUTHOR

Ryan Gale is an artist and writer from Minnesota who spends summers freshwater fishing with his son.

Contents

CHAPTER ONE

A Favorite Place to Fish

The sun was rising when Louis and his parents reached their favorite fishing spot. It was a small freshwater lake with a **public** fishing **dock**. Louis carried his equipment to the end of the dock. He had a fishing pole and tackle box, where he stored his fishing gear. He also had a box of worms for **bait**.

Louis got a hook from his tackle box. He attached it to the end of the string, or line, on his fishing pole. Then he put some metal sinkers on the line. This would make the bait sink in the water. Next, Louis attached a plastic bobber to the line. The bobber would float on the water's surface, keeping the bait from hitting the bottom of the lake. Louis positioned the bobber so it would keep the bait at a depth where fish might be. Then he used his fishing pole to throw, or cast, the line into the water. He watched the bobber. If a fish ate his bait, it would pull the bobber underwater.

Fish such as bass often hide in the shade beneath a dock's wooden beams. To catch these fish, many people fish from docks or piers.

Fishing requires patience, time, and focus. People must stay alert so they can be prepared to act when a fish bites.

Louis waited patiently. Suddenly, his bobber began bouncing up and down. A fish was biting the bait! Then the bobber shot underwater. Louis felt a fish tugging on his fishing line. He jerked his pole so the hook stuck in the fish's mouth. Then he turned the crank on the pole to **reel** in the fish. Louis pulled a large sunfish onto the dock.

Louis carefully took the hook out of the fish's mouth to avoid harming the creature. He smiled, holding the fish so his dad could take a picture. Then Louis gently put the fish back in the lake. Some people keep the fish they catch for food. But Louis's family practices catch and release. They catch fish and then let them go. This helps keep fish populations stable.

The United States has many freshwater lakes and rivers. These bodies of water provide **habitats** for many fish. For thousands of years, freshwater fish have been an important food source for people in North America. Today, people of all ages go freshwater fishing. It is a fun sport to enjoy alone or with friends and family.

FISH STOCKING

Some US state governments add fish to lakes and rivers. This practice is called fish stocking. Fish are raised on fish farms across the country. When the fish are still young, they are released into lakes and rivers. The fish grow up in the new habitats. Fish stocking helps promote fishing by ensuring that there are always plenty of fish for people to catch.

CHAPTER TWO

Freshwater Fishing Basics

There are many places in the United States for **anglers** to go freshwater fishing. The country has millions of freshwater lakes. This includes the five Great Lakes, which are Lake Superior, Lake Michigan, Lake Huron, Lake Erie, and Lake Ontario. They are among the largest freshwater lakes in the world. The United States also has more than 3.5 million miles (5.6 million km) of rivers.

Anglers often fish in lakes and rivers from the shore. Many lakes and rivers have public fishing docks. Docks used for loading and unloading boats can also be used for fishing. Some anglers fish from boats, which are helpful for fishing over large areas and reaching **remote** spots. Frozen rivers and lakes can be fished by drilling holes in the ice. This is called ice fishing.

Anglers on the Great Lakes can catch fish such as pike (pictured), muskie, bass, and walleye.

To stay safe while ice fishing, anglers should wear warm winter clothing and waterproof boots.

Freshwater lakes and rivers contain many types of fish. Some popular types include bluegill, bass, walleye, northern pike, catfish, trout, and salmon. Some fish, such as bluegill and bass, are found throughout the United States. Others are found only in certain areas. For example, walleye and northern pike are found in northern states.

Freshwater fish have different characteristics. It's useful for anglers to be able to identify them. That way, anglers know what type of fish they caught.

FLY FISHING

Fly fishing is a popular fishing method in the United States. It involves using a type of fake bait called a fly. Flies often look like insects. They float on the water's surface. This makes them ideal for fishing in shallow rivers and creeks. Fly fishing can be done from a boat, but many anglers prefer to wade into the water. They wear waterproof pants called waders to stay dry. Unlike other fishing rods, fly fishing rods are longer and thinner. They also use thicker line.

Freshwater anglers can choose from several different fishing methods. Bobber fishing is one of the most popular methods. It involves using a bobber to suspend bait underwater. Trolling is another method. It involves casting bait into the water and slowly reeling it in. Fish become interested in the bait's movement. Some anglers prefer trolling from a boat. Bait is cast from a slow-moving boat and pulled behind it.

Catching fish requires skill and patience. Anglers must know where fish live and what they eat. They must also have the right equipment and know how to use it. Kids and beginners can take fishing classes to learn more. The internet is a useful tool for finding fishing classes and fishing spots.

Experienced anglers can help beginners improve their fishing skills and learn new techniques.

CHAPTER THREE

Freshwater Fishing Gear

To catch freshwater fish, anglers need the right kind of bait. Some anglers use live bait. This includes worms such as nightcrawlers and leeches. It also includes small fish such as minnows. Anglers can use many minnow **species**, including suckers. People put the bait on their fishing hooks. When a fish bites the bait, the hook sticks in its mouth.

Many anglers use fake bait such as plastic worms. Unlike live bait, fake bait can often be reused. Lures are one type of fake bait. They are usually made of metal or plastic. Anglers use fishing poles to make lures move in different ways. This movement attracts fish. Lures are often brightly colored to make them easier for fish to see.

Anglers also need fishing poles. Fishing poles have reels for winding line back in. They come in different sizes. Short fishing poles are used for ice fishing. They are often used by kids, too. Long fishing poles are thick and strong. They are used for catching big fish species such as northern pike.

Anglers learn how to tie different fishing knots, such as the clinch knot. They use these knots to prepare their fishing rods for casting and attach lures to their hooks.

There are many types of fishing lures. Some move in unique ways to attract fish. Others look like live bait.

Many anglers fish from boats. Fishing boats often have seats for sitting and flat floors for standing. They sometimes have large motors with propellers to make them move. Boats with small motors move more slowly. These boats are used for trolling.

For ice fishing, anglers need special equipment. An **auger** is a tool used to cut holes in the ice. Augers have sharp blades that spin like a drill. This creates a hole in the ice that an angler can fish from. Some people sit inside ice houses while ice fishing.

These are small shelters that protect anglers from the wind. Many ice houses have heaters to keep people warm.

Anglers can buy bait and fishing equipment at sporting goods stores. Some businesses rent fishing gear, too. Bait shops are often located near popular fishing spots. Anglers can search online or at a library to decide which bait and equipment to use.

In some states, boaters are required to get a boating license and take boat safety courses. This helps anglers stay safe while fishing on the water.

CHAPTER FOUR

Safety and Sportsmanship

To avoid accidents, anglers must fish safely. They should always keep their hooks and lures away from other people's skin. They should be aware of their surroundings when casting to avoid hitting other people. It is also important for anglers to safely handle fish. Some fish have sharp teeth and pointy fins that can injure anglers. Handling fish gently helps keep fish from being harmed, too.

To stay safe, kids and beginners should go fishing with an experienced adult. When fishing from a boat, anglers should wear life jackets. These help people float if they fall into the water. When ice fishing, anglers must wait until the ice is thick enough to hold people without breaking. At least 4 inches (10 cm) of ice is needed to safely ice fish.

Anglers should also wear the right clothing. In summer, wearing a hat and sunscreen helps prevent sunburn. Ice fishers should wear winter clothing to stay warm. Many anglers also wear sunglasses to help reduce the sun's glare on water, ice, and snow.

Anglers should be gentle when removing hooks from a fish's mouth. To avoid injuring the fish, the angler should try to remove the hook as quickly and carefully as possible.

There are many rules anglers must follow, too. Rules differ from state to state. An angler should know her state's rules before going fishing. In most states, people ages 16 or older need a license to fish. Anglers may only be able to keep fish that are certain sizes. They may be allowed to keep a limited number of fish. Some fish can only be caught during specific times of year. These rules protect fish populations by making sure they don't get too small. This allows young fish to grow up and reproduce.

Whether fishing from a large boat or a small canoe, anglers should always wear life jackets to stay safe.

When releasing a fish, an angler should hold it upright and briefly keep it underwater. This helps the fish recover before it swims away.

Anglers should also practice good sportsmanship. This means acting in a fair, responsible way. To do this, anglers should follow fishing rules. They should respect other anglers and the fish they catch. They should also avoid causing fish stress or harm. Unless anglers intend to eat the fish they catch, they should return the fish to the water as quickly as possible. By following rules and practicing good sportsmanship, anglers can help make fishing enjoyable for everyone.

GLOSSARY

anglers (AN-glurz) Anglers are people who fish with a hook and line. Many anglers fish in freshwater rivers and lakes.

auger (AW-gur) An auger is a tool for drilling holes. Anglers can use an auger to drill holes in the ice for ice fishing.

bait (BAYT) Bait is something anglers put on a fishing hook and use to attract fish. Common types of bait include worms, minnows, and lures.

dock (DOK) A dock is a platform for loading and unloading boats. People decided to fish from the dock.

habitats (HAB-ih-tats) Habitats are places where plants and animals live. Lakes and rivers provide habitats for many types of fish.

public (PUB-lik) When something is public, it is open to all people. Many lakes and rivers have public fishing docks.

reel (REEL) To reel in a fish means to pull it in with a fishing rod by winding in or letting out fishing line. The angler used her fishing rod to reel in the fish.

remote (reh-MOHT) When something is remote, it is far away or out of the way. Some anglers use boats to reach remote areas.

species (SPEE-sheez) A species is a group of living things that share the same traits. Anglers can use many minnow species as bait.

FAST FACTS

- There are millions of freshwater lakes and rivers in the United States. Many types of fish live in these bodies of water.
- Popular freshwater fish include bass, walleye, northern pike, bluegill, and catfish.
- There are several types of freshwater fishing, including fly fishing and ice fishing. Anglers can also use different methods such as trolling and bobber fishing.
- Anglers can use live bait or fake bait to catch fish. Worms and minnows are popular types of live bait. Some anglers prefer fake bait such as lures.
- Fishing lures move in different ways when pulled through the water. They are often brightly colored to attract fish.
- By following fishing rules, anglers can help protect fish populations. Anglers must understand the size limits in their area and practice good sportsmanship. In some states, they must have fishing licenses.

ONE STRIDE FURTHER

- If you were freshwater fishing, would you use live bait or fake bait? Why?
- What are some ways you can help protect freshwater fish populations?
- What are some ways to practice good fishing sportsmanship that aren't mentioned in this book?

FIND OUT MORE

IN THE LIBRARY

MacCarald, Clara. *Fly Fishing*. Parker, CO: The Child's World, 2024.

Mazzarella, Kerri. *Ice Fishing*. New York, NY: Crabtree, 2023.

Paxton, John. *My Awesome Guide to Freshwater Fishing: Essential Techniques and Tools for Kids*. Emeryville, CA: Rockridge Press, 2021.

ON THE WEB

Visit our website for links about freshwater fishing:
childsworld.com/links

Note to Parents, Caregivers, Teachers, and Librarians: We routinely verify our Web links to make sure they are safe and active sites. So encourage your readers to check them out!

INDEX